ENDANGERED PREDATORS

ENDANGERED
PREDATORS

BY JOHN HARRIS AND
ALETA PAHL

ILLUSTRATED BY ALETA PAHL

CONCEIVED AND PRODUCED BY
WHITEHALL, HADLYME & SMITH, INC.

DOUBLEDAY & COMPANY, INC., GARDEN CITY, NEW YORK

Library of Congress Cataloging in Publication Data

Harris, John, 1935–
Endangered Predators.

Bibliography: p. 83.
SUMMARY: Five stories of predatory animals, the
wolf, fox, coyote, cougar, and bobcat, stressing the
importance of predators to the balance of nature.
1. Rare animals—North America—Juvenile literature.
2. Predatory animals—Juvenile literature.
[1. Rare animals.   2. Predatory animals]   I. Pahl,
Aleta, joint author.   II. Title.
QL83.H37   599'.74428
ISBN 0-385-08038-7 Trade
ISBN 0-385-08012-3 Prebound
Library of Congress Catalog Card Number 75–34051

Contents

Acknowledgments

John Harris and I would like to thank the following people for their help and encouragement. Thanks go to Dr. Michael Fox and Hope Ryden for their very generous and helpful advice. Our deepest appreciation goes to Tony Nocera for all the years of work for predators.

I must personally thank all my friends and two special people: Charlie Ericksen, whose island at the edge of the wilderness gave me a feeling for what I was drawing and describing, and John Lillstrom, my source of confidence.

ALETA PAHL

ENDANGERED PREDATORS

PREFACE

WHY WOULD ANYONE TAKE TWO TIMBER WOLVES IN A run-down old van and travel across thirty-eight states and parts of Canada? I think that for me it had something to do with justice. I had found fairness hard to find for myself, but then I discovered an animal that was in worse shape than I was. It was the wolf. Like all wildlife, a wolf cannot speak for itself. It cannot stand up for its rights. It was easy to see that after everything man has been doing to wolves and other wild animals, they really deserve more fairness and justice.

Wild animals once lived throughout the wilderness playing their important part in the natural balance. The deer, the moose, and the wolf all lived together, each in its own way. Each was important to the others and to the whole environment. For thousands of years this balance was kept, but then white settlers came into the wilderness, forever pushing deeper and deeper. And where they came, they cut the trees and changed the wilderness. The wildlife was either killed or driven farther into the wilds. In only two or three hundred years, so much wilderness and wildlife have been destroyed that some animals have become extinct—there are none left. There are other animals that could soon become extinct because there are so few of them left. And once an animal becomes extinct, we cannot ever bring it back.

It seemed to me that more people needed to be aware of the trouble these animals were in. There are many conservation organizations and many good magazines that distribute information to a large audience. But to me, the best way to get across the message was to go to the schools and talk to the children who would one day be running this country. If their attitudes could be changed and they could be made to care, then there would be hope for the wolf and other wildlife.

So in 1969 I started doing educational programs in California where I lived. I had obtained an 88-pound timber wolf by the name of Jethro. Someone had had him as a pet—something people should never do with a wild animal, especially a wolf. Wolves cannot be housebroken or trained like a dog. A wolf is too much of a free spirit. He is too much a part of all that makes up a wilderness.

Jethro was a very different wolf. He didn't mind people surrounding him or petting him. A wolf in the wild will run from people as fast as he can. But I was able to take Jethro into schools or wherever else I gave my program. The more programs I did, the more Jethro enjoyed the attention. He became a real ham after a while. Soon I added Clem to my group. He was a 110-pound Alaskan wolf. Clem was always shier than Jethro, but even he was a remarkable wolf.

The whole point of my program was, and still is, to bring a real live wolf to the people, especially the kids, and give them a feeling for what they should be trying to protect. Usually I had volunteers on the road with me to do the speaking and help handle the wolves. Wherever we traveled, we showed the Canadian film *Death of a Legend*—a really beautiful movie about the behavior of wolves throughout the centuries. After the film, we brought in Jethro and Clem and discussed the problems facing much of our wildlife and what could be done to help.

We brought a wolf into a school and even into a classroom and let the kids touch and pet him. Here he was, a beautiful, big strong animal that could easily crush the bones of children in his jaws, but an animal that wanted only to lick their faces. Children could see that Jethro was not like the wolf that chased Little Red Ridinghood. Jethro represented real life and the kids could learn an important lesson in the difference between fairy tales and the reality they lived in.

After meeting a wolf and learning from our program that these animals were still hunted, poisoned, and shot, the kids were always anxious to help save wolves—to help Jethro's wild brothers. Even as children, they could help, and help a lot. We talked about laws and about how laws could help protect wildlife as they do people. We had no trouble encouraging the children to write to senators, representatives, and to the President supporting conservation bills in Congress. The kids would then go home and tell their parents that they had pet a wolf and that wolves were not bad and that we should not shoot them or wear their fur coats.

Wherever we went, the program was successful, and more and more schools wanted us to visit. Meanwhile, we had shocked the wolf experts by being able to bring a wolf into a building on a leash. We were shocking teachers and principals by letting the kids pet and hug our wolf. And we were shocking Congress by the mail sent as a result of our program. All in all, we were having quite an effect wherever we went. Newspapers began writing articles about us and Jethro became a TV star in some towns.

Sometimes we did receive a little criticism from people. Some thought it was cruel to keep Clem and Jethro in a van or on a heavy chain. We explained that the chain was more for us than for the wolf. A wolf is three times as strong as any dog and Clem and Jethro could really pull their chains. The bigger chain did not cut into our hands as much as a smaller one.

We also explained that first of all, Jethro and Clem were not our pets. They were not even really tame. We called them socialized, which meant that they had become used to a lot of people around them and had even grown to enjoy all the attention. Even though Clem and Jethro would have been happier roaming free in the wilderness, the good they were doing with the program was helping all of their wild brothers.

Jethro and Clem were wildlife ambassadors. They brought a piece of wilderness with them to people throughout the country. They showed people what should be protected. Clem and Jethro were not unhappy either. We did not force them to do anything they wouldn't do. You cannot force a wolf.

Sometimes it seemed that you could actually see Jethro smiling. He must have enjoyed being loved and being a star and he especially loved the little kids. Sometimes you would swear that he posed for the photographers, who loved to get pictures of a little girl next to a wolf whose head looked twice as big as hers.

Jethro and Clem are dead now. Someone poisoned them one July night in 1973 in Brooklyn, New York. It was an utterly senseless murder. Afterward, everyone encouraged me to continue my programs. And I figured that Jethro and Clem had affected so many thousands of people that I had to make sure that it all hadn't been for nothing. So I found another wolf—a nephew of Jethro by the name of Rocky—and we began again. Rocky was very young, but even then he showed signs of becoming as good as his uncle had been. Rocky looks more and more like Jethro as he gets older.

Jethro, Clem, and now Rocky bring the issue of conservation right to the people. Rocky makes them aware of what they have been doing to endanger our wildlife, and he encourages the children he meets to ask what they can do to help now, and how they can make a career in some field of conservation. And there are many different types of work anyone can do.

Some people want to study how wolves or other animals behave. The study of behavior is called ethology and students can study to be ethologists. Many then can go out into the wilderness to study an animal in its natural environment. Others can work in laboratories, more like scientists. There are jobs as forest rangers and game wardens where one can live in a wild area and look after the forest and the wildlife and enforce the regulations there. There are many other jobs in government that deal with wildlife. Sometimes surveys are taken on animal populations and on migrations. Sometimes animals are tagged so that they can be found again and it can be known where they went and what they did.

There are other ways that people can help in wildlife conservation. A lot can be done by forming a conservation organization. It can even be started in school as a club. Speakers can be brought in and money can be raised to help certain projects.

Sometimes it is hard to decide what you want to do right now. But while you are deciding, it is a good idea to stay in school. Then it is easier to find the area of study that you would like best. And while you are studying, you can join a club or group of people who feel the same about conservation. Together you can let others know about the threats to our wildlife.

Wolves to me are a symbol of wilderness. After working with wolves and studying their behavior for several years, I know them to be one of the most intelligent and interesting animals. I felt it was wrong for so many people to want to kill these animals or want to wear their fur. Some people might say that this is a personal opinion. Others might say that they just don't care about wolves. But protecting our wildlife is more than an opinion when you study nature and how animals live together—how everything is connected. These are all scientific facts. And man is just a part of that system. When we kill off an animal or pollute or destroy part of our earth, it is going to hurt us sooner or later. The wolf is a symbol of all of the misunderstanding that many people have had toward many animals. A wolf is a predator. He must kill for his food. Some people don't like to see deer being eaten by wolves. They think that it is terrible and cruel. Yet they will eat venison, which is part of a dead deer.

Wolves cannot go down to their local grocery store for

supplies. Wild animals depend upon each other for food, and those animals that are weak or sick become useful food for other animals. In our programs and talks with school children we always try to make it clear that predators such as the wolf are not mean and terrible. They should not be feared or hated. Wolves, cougars, coyotes, foxes, bobcats, and others must kill other weaker and sick animals for their own survival.

If Rocky can show students and adults the importance of a wolf as a predator, then all the other predators such as cougars and coyotes will benefit. The importance of predators is what this book is about. Although we take Rocky all over the United States and Canada, it is impossible to get to see every school and every child. Sometimes a book such as this can reach many more people. They can read it and learn about nature and how predators live. If they understand animals, they will have no need to fear or hate them. Instead they will know that the animal has a purpose and an important role to play on this earth.

Life is precious in all of its forms. All must be respected. All forms are connected. Each life is important, not only in itself, but in its relationship to other lives. Each individual life is part of the whole. Because all living things depend upon each other, some animals must die so that others may live. After millions of years of evolution, nature has insured the survival of its species by a chain of relationships. All animals have become members of naturally balanced systems. In each of these ecosystems, the species of animals live together with the soil, air, water, and plants. But there is only a certain amount of food. If animals such as deer and rabbits who eat plants become too numerous, there will not be enough food for all. To make sure the numbers of these animals are kept in balance, a system of predation has evolved. The job of keeping certain species in check has been given to the predator—the animal that kills for his food.

Instead of writing this as a science or biology book with lists of facts about each predator, it is written as a series of stories. This way it is easier to get into the skin of the animal and to help explain why it does the things it does. In the next chapters, the animals Chinook and Metayo, Tawney, Yip, Torch, and Smokie are not real. They are made-up characters, but they could be real because their stories could be the stories of any real-life predator.

In many other books, a wolf or cougar is often shown as the bad animal—the killer. But this time the predator is shown as he exists in nature. The only bad animal in these chapters is man, for the cruel things he has done to our predators. Perhaps when everyone reads about these predators and understands the problems these animals are facing, old attitudes can be changed and people can join together to help preserve and protect their wild brother—the predator.

CHINOOK

YOUNG FLINT, A GRAY SHADOW IN THE NORTHERN LIGHTS, stood silently beside his sister. Their fur glistened in the moonlight. The stars blazed across the sky and the night air was still. No breeze stirred the pines. The silence was broken by a lone wailing howl from across the open white stretch of the hidden snow-covered lake. Young Flint lifted his nose to the sky and answered the call. Tonight he and Mist were joining the rest of the wolf pack. Several days had passed since the pack split up in search of food. The young wolves started off through the deep snow. Old Chip followed. He was like an uncle to the yearling wolves, help-

ing to show them how to survive their first winter. All three wolves bounded through the drifts, anxious to see the rest of the pack. Where the snow was very deep, they walked in single file with Mist and Old Chip stepping into the tracks of Young Flint who broke the way. In only a short time there was a happy reunion with seven members of the wolf pack circling each other, brushing shoulders, wagging tails, and licking faces. It was an exciting occasion.

The leader of the pack was Chinook. He was the largest and strongest member. Chinook had become leader, or dominant male, of the pack two years before when his father, Rocky, had been killed. An airplane had come down out of the sky one day as the pack crossed an ice-covered lake. The wolves had raced toward the forest when they heard the cracking shots from the hunter's rifle. But before the pack was able to reach the shelter of the pine trees, three of the wolves were shot. One of them was Rocky. Chinook, once safe within the trees, had stopped to look back. He watched the roaring plane land and the man walk over to the blood-stained snow. The hunter took out his knife that flashed in the sunlight and cut into the dead wolves, stripping them of their fur. The entire nightmare had lasted only a few minutes and then the plane was gone and once again there was silence. Chinook and the rest of the pack never forgot what the sound of planes meant. The roaring metal birds brought death to any wolf who could not quickly seek the shelter of the thick woods.

But tonight all the wolves were together again. Because Chinook was their leader, Young Flint and Mist and even Old Chip nuzzled his mouth and licked his face. Chinook stood still and accepted their friendly greetings. He held his tail high, while the others wagged their tails. This was a sign that he was the head of the pack. Chinook's coat of thick fur was pale under the moonlight and its silver tips gleamed. Mist was so excited that she ran up to Chinook and rolled over on her back in the snow. She was letting him know that she respected his leadership.

After much greeting and friendliness, the wolves broke into a chorus of howls. The eerie wails echoed through the forest. This was part of the ceremony before the hunt—a general get-together. When the songfest was over, the seven wolves ran off along the edge of the lake in an easy graceful trot. They could keep this pace up for hours. Above them to the north, the northern lights zigzagged and flickered across the heavens. It was bitter cold, but the wolves did not feel it. They were protected during the winter months under thick and long fur coats. Tonight the snow-covered lakes became short cuts to the trees on the far shore. Very often in their hunts, the wolves came across deer and moose who walked out onto the lake to escape the huge drifts of snow in the forests.

In the winter months, Chinook's pack had to rely on deer and moose for most of their food. Beavers were safe in the dams beneath the ice, and the weasels, rabbits, and mice escaped along runways beneath the snow into their burrows and tunnels. For the wolves, it was not an easy job to kill a moose that weighed twelve times as much as they did, and whose hoofs could easily kill one of them. Sometimes they found bodies of deer that had starved to death. Young Flint and Mist had found a deer only three days before, trapped in the deep snow. The unfortunate young doe was slowly dying of starvation. She was killed instantly by Young Flint. Tonight, with the entire pack together again, perhaps they could bring down a moose. Yet when the wolves hunted there were always many attempts and failures before a successful kill.

Tonight the pack was lucky. An old and weak bull moose was spotted. If a moose stood his ground and faced his attackers, the wolves would have to give up and find an easier victim. But this moose ran instead of facing Chinook and the others. The pack was able to bring him down. If the wolves had not killed this moose, he would have died anyway from the disease that was making him weak. Now the moose served an important purpose. He became food for Chinook's pack. In turn, the wolves were helping the moose population to stay healthy and strong by eliminating the weak, the sick, and the old. Only the healthiest moose survived to produce healthy calves in the spring. Chinook's pack of wolves lived in a natural balance with the moose and the deer in their territory. Each species helped the other.

As the pack's leader, Chinook was the first to eat. Metayo, the dominant female of the pack, ate with him. The rest waited their turn and they understood this. The wolves with the lowest standing in the pack ate last. Bounder was the weakest wolf of the pack and could be pushed around by everyone else. She usually grabbed the leftover scraps. When the wolves finished their dinner, the eastern horizon was already growing light. Clouds moved in. And within minutes, the air was white with snowflakes. Chinook and Metayo lay down several feet apart in the snow. The rest of

the pack was also tired and before the sun rose, each wolf was curled up into a tight ball of thick fur. Their only unprotected spot was their nose, so each hid his nose under his curled bushy tail. Young Flint was so tired he slept for hours without moving. The snow continued to fall and became a warm white blanket to the sleeping wolves.

By the middle of February, there was a growing excitement within the pack. It was the beginning of the six-week mating period. Each male wolf busied himself with impressing his favorite female. And the female wolves flirted among their favorite male wolves. Yet as pack leader and as the dominant male wolf, Chinook tried to prevent any of the lower wolves from mating. It was the way of the pack that only the strongest wolves could mate. As dominant female, Metayo was the one to have pups. Although she flirted with Rusty, the wolf who ranked second to Chinook, Rusty preferred little Bounder. The year before, while Chinook was kept busy keeping order in the pack, Metayo had mated with Rusty. He was Young Flint and Mist's father. Yet when the pups were born, Chinook, as pack leader, behaved as though he were their real father and took care of them. This year, Chinook succeeded in his efforts to keep Rusty away from Metayo. As the strongest pair of wolves in the pack, Chinook and Metayo would produce the healthiest pups.

By April there was a hint of warmth in the air as the sun climbed higher. Smells and sounds began to fill the forest. The smell of pine and balsam trees and the sound of melting ice were all signs of early spring in the wilderness world of Chinook's pack. Snowbanks were sinking and disappearing. One morning, Chinook opened his eyes and uncurled his tail. The sun was bright and the ice and snow on many of the lakes had melted. The reflections of pine trees could once again be seen in the clear cold blue water.

Once more, water lapped against the rocky shores. From across the lake, a call of laughter was heard by the wolves as loons landed on the water.

Chinook stood up and looked around him. Young Flint and Mist were roughhousing and playing a game of tag and ambush. Bounder was sniffing the newly exposed brown surface where snow had melted. Rusty was standing on a ledge looking down into a clear pool of water where the fins of trout shone in the sun beneath the lake's surface. Old Chip was still sleeping. Metayo was busy. She spent the day digging a new den. The sixty-three days of wait for the pups to arrive was nearing an end. She had spent many days digging a tunnel angling down into a sandy hill only a few yards away from last year's den. At the end of the tunnel, she dug out a clearing. With the den completed and ready, Metayo now relaxed and awaited her pups.

By May, amid the singing of chickadees, the return of ducks, the call of the killdeer, and the opening of spring flowers, the wolf pups were born. Beside Metayo lay five dark brown wiggling furry balls with short legs, snub noses, and rat-like tails. Each pup weighed one pound and its eyes would not open until it was about two weeks old. Wolf pups were born at this gentle time of year when they would have the best chance of survival. They could have time to grow and learn how to survive before the harshness of winter.

During the first two weeks, Metayo remained in the den almost all the time, nursing the hungry pups. Chinook and the rest of the pack brought food to her. Because the den was close to water, Metayo could easily and quickly step outside for a drink. During these first days, not even Chinook was allowed inside the den. Finally one day after the third week, he was allowed to crouch and crawl down into the den and watch the furry bodies pawing and licking each other, and chewing one another's ears. The pups were beginning to play. Before long they would be trying to wobble out of the den, curious about the light at the end of the tunnel.

The birth of pups is always a great event in a wolf pack, and Bounder, Rusty, and Old Chip were highly excited. Young Flint and Mist were somewhat curious of the whimpering sounds they heard coming from the den. All the wolves waited anxiously for the pups finally to stumble outside.

One morning, Dark, the biggest and darkest of the litter, pushed his nose out the den's entrance and looked around. His eyes were still blue. It would take a few more weeks before they turned into a golden yellow like his parents. Dark's sisters, Tundra and Firn, also looked out of the tunnel. The fourth pup, Nemo, was not so sure about this brand-new world of sights and smells, and he stayed within the shadow of the hole. The fifth pup had grown steadily weaker after birth and had died. As the pups took their first wobbly steps, the adult wolves jostled and shouldered each other and whined. All watched Dark stumble over a twig and Tundra sniff at a blade of grass. Nemo finally emerged from the den, but whimpered when he could not see his mother, Metayo, any more. Firn stumbled and rolled down part of the hillside.

Chinook carefully watched his pups and when he saw Firn too far away from the den, he picked her up by taking her whole body in his jaws. Her head and forelegs hung out one side of his mouth and her hind legs hung out the other side.

Chinook played a big role as father now. As Metayo's milk supply became inadequate for the growing pups, Chinook brought back fresh meat after a hunt. Because it was too difficult to carry chunks of meat all the way back to the den,

Chinook carried meat back in his stomach, half digested. Then he could regurgitate it for the pups. The wolf pups soon learned that by biting and pulling at his mouth, they could make him cough up food for them. Now Metayo was spending less and less time in the den. One evening she joined the pack in their howl before the hunt. But instead of returning to her den and pups, she ran off with the wolves. Rusty was left behind to baby-sit.

The following morning Metayo and Chinook moved their pups to another location. The original den was no longer big enough for the growing pups. Their legs had become almost a foot long and their feet looked too big for their bodies. Their ears were growing larger and longer. The new location became an outdoor headquarters for the wolves, where they rested, played, and brought food for the pups until they were able to travel to the sites of the kills.

Metayo chose a grassy area with a good view of their surrounding territory. Here, Dark and the other pups were able to play and learn about their new surroundings. Tundra soon learned to use tall clumps of grass as hiding places where she could lie in wait to ambush Firn. Chinook always patiently allowed Dark and the others to bite his tail. If the pups' games ever got too rough, Chinook interrupted them. All of the pack members patiently allowed the pups to wrestle and climb over them.

One of the most important things the pups were learning was discipline from Chinook. Just as the rest of the pack showed respect for Chinook, the pups learned to obey him respectfully. Yet because they were only pups, Chinook and the other adults were lenient with them. The pups learned that a direct stare from their parents or a snarl and a growl could be followed by Chinook taking their snout in his mouth and pinning them to the ground. Within the litter itself, positions were established. Dark became the leader in the litter. One day to show his dominance, he scampered around with a leg bone of a deer in his mouth until the long bone became too heavy for him and he lost interest in it.

During the August days of midsummer, as the pups' playfulness prepared them for the skills they would later need to survive, the rest of the pack found hunting more difficult than during the spring. The fawns were older and larger and escaped more easily. Many of the weak and diseased animals had already been taken by the wolves. Now they relied on smaller animals such as beaver, rabbits, squirrels, weasels, and even mice.

One afternoon, after chasing each other in games of tag and ambush, the pups heard the howls of the pack. The adults were returning from the hunt. Dark ran to meet Chinook and pulled at his mouth until his father regurgitated the fresh meat for him. Metayo brought back an extra thigh and leg bone from the deer. She buried the bone by digging a hole with her forepaws and then pushing back the dirt with her nose. The food could be saved until later and the bones could be bitten into smaller bits by Metayo for her pups. Although Dark and the other pups were beginning to look more and more like their parents, they still had their baby teeth. Replacing these teeth with their permanent ones was one of the last steps toward maturity.

As summer changed into fall, the pups' tails became brushy and more wolf-like. Their coats were lighter colored and thicker. Dark, Tundra, and the others developed their curiosity about small moving animals, such as mice and frogs, into a method of obtaining their own food. More and more often, the pups were led to the sites of the kills. Slowly they learned the extent and features of the pack's territory—an area that covered about ten square miles for each wolf. Gradually the pups became integrated into the society of the pack. They had to obey all the other members of the pack until they developed more strength and skill and, perhaps, could dominate some of the older members. Already Dark was pushing his brother and sisters around. Soon it would be easy for him to dominate the weakest wolf, little Bounder. Yet it would take many months before he could become boss over Rusty, Mist, or Young Flint.

The fall became a joyful time for Chinook and his pack. The deer and other prey animals had become fat after feeding throughout the summer. Beavers were easily caught because they spent more time away from their dams to cut and move logs before the lakes froze. The leaves fell by mid-October and the woods became drenched in shades of gold.

One night as the wolves gathered for a howl beneath a

golden maple, the moonlight streamed through the branches and the pack was bathed in a golden light. It was that night that the pups went out on their first hunt. Dark and Tundra even helped pull down a young deer.

Because wolves are running animals, they must kill on the run and also avoid the sharp hoofs. Chinook attacked the deer's most vulnerable spot—its abdominal area in front of the hind legs. The deer died quickly as the successful tears at his stomach spilled his intestines on the ground. The deer had tried to outrun Chinook but ran right into the rest of the pack. With a bluff on one side of it and the wolves on the other, the deer could not escape.

When the pack finished their shares of the kill and moved off into the forest, a lone fox searched for meager leftovers. The next morning an eagle picked the carcass clean.

While the forest was alive with activity in preparation for winter, the wolves' only preparation was the growth of their heavy winter coats. Flocks of birds formed for migrations, frogs burrowed deep into the mud, squirrels gathered nuts, and the night skies were often filled with the honking of geese as their V-formations could be seen silhouetted against the autumn moon. One day the surface of the lake was stirred by a north wind. For the mallards and other ducks still remaining, it was a warning that winter was on its way.

One morning Firn woke up and found that the ground was dusted with snow. After examining this new happening and seeing that it was not to be feared, Firn and Tundra played in the white wet stuff. Nemo scampered along the ground with his nose in the snow. For the moment, the coming of winter was a new playland for the pups, but soon the harshness of the winter months would test their ability and strength. Many wolf pups never make it through their first winter. A brother of Young Flint died the winter before when, caught off guard, he was kicked by a moose. A weak sister died of starvation. This winter, Dark, Tundra, Firn, and Nemo would have to put to use all they had learned from the months of roughhousing, stalking, and ambushing each other in play.

In only a few more days the landscape was engulfed in a carpet of snow. Once again, ice was groaning as it formed on the lakes and branches snapped under the weight of snow. Soon the wolves again would feed on the starving deer. Again the pack would hunt moose. This year Chinook's pack began the winter with eleven wolves. Last year they had lost four members, and this year just as many could die.

Aside from injury or starvation, the wolves' greatest threat was man. The great metal birds from out of the sky

were to be feared. Most of the pack stayed as far away from man as possible, but the pups would still need to learn this. Alone in their wilderness home, if left undisturbed by the hunters with their poisons, traps, and guns, the family of wolves could live out their lives as part of the natural balance. They belonged there.

As Chinook, Metayo, and the rest once again gathered for a chorus of howls, their wailing calls echoed and floated on the wind through the snowy wilds. Once again the wolves trotted off through the snow, until their grayish, ghostlike forms disappeared through the pines.

TAWNEY

Tawney lay relaxed, soaking up the sunlight. Her golden eyes were mere slits as she half-slept, half-gazed out at the valley and meadows below her rocky ledge. A few flies buzzed around her and she twitched the end of her long, heavy tail and flicked her small ears to discourage them. Her long, slender body almost blended into the color of the rocks and ground around her. Only the black tip of her tail, the black on the back of her ears, and the black outline to her white muzzle differed from the tans and cream colorings of her sleek fur that gleamed in the sunlight. The very tip of the cougar's nose was a light pink.

High above the quiet canyon amid the mountains, soared a golden eagle searching the meadows far below for a ground squirrel or rabbit. As the huge eagle dipped his powerful wings, they reflected the sun's bright light. His occasional screeching did not bother Tawney. She rested her

round head on her forepaws and went to sleep. It was late summer and the hot and dry afternoons made most of the animals who lived in these valleys and mountains drowsy. A light breeze rustled the leaves of the young aspen tree a few feet away from the sleeping cougar.

Earlier that morning, Tawney killed a mule deer after it watchfully stepped outside the safety of the forest and began to walk across a grassy meadow. The meadow was a clearing in the forest where several years before, a forest fire had destroyed the large fir trees. Now young aspen trees grew here and, where the meadow bordered a stream, there were willow trees. Deer liked to come down to the stream to drink and feed on the tender willow leaves.

That morning Tawney patiently watched the young deer cross the clearing. It flicked its tail and ears and looked up again and again, ever alert for danger. Tawney then silently crept through the tall grass on her large padded feet, using large rocks or fallen tree trunks to help hide her slow and careful stalk. When the doe was within fifty yards, Tawney sprang onto the deer's shoulders and killed it instantly with a bite into the back of the neck. The victim had time to hear only a rushing sound and catch a blur of motion as she was struck down by a hundred pounds of strength.

The quiet, but deadly, event barely disrupted the life of the meadow and forest. Birds continued to chirp and sing. A porcupine lumbered across the far side of the meadow and climbed a tree, hungry for the inner bark. Tawney dragged her deer into the shade of the forest and used her sharp claws to rip open the doe's belly. She began by eating the parts she liked best—the liver, heart, and lungs. When Tawney had eaten her fill, she carefully covered her kill with dirt, leaves, and some small branches to protect the meat from flies and insects. It then remained fresh and she could return later to eat more. The deer would not go to waste. Whatever Tawney did not eat, coyotes, foxes, bears, or even eagles would finish.

So, with a full stomach, Tawney peacefully slept away the hot afternoon. That evening as darkness settled over the canyon, bullfrogs began their croaking in a nearby pond in the valley below. Tawney stretched and arched her back. She began to wander through much of the over twenty square miles she knew as home. This was her territory. Several years before, when she was two years old, Tawney had been forced to leave her mother's territory. Her mother had come into heat again, ready to raise a new family. So Tawney and her brother left their mother to search out territories of their own. Tawney found this wild and rugged canyon with enough deer, rabbits, beavers, and porcupines to feed her. She always avoided other cougars and their territories except during mating season.

As Tawney crossed over some of her home range, she once again left scrapes—piles of dirt, leaves, or pine needles with her droppings buried in it. These scrapes, along with spraying bushes, rocks, and trees, marked her territory to other cougars, telling them that this was her home. In her wanderings Tawney could travel up to twenty miles in one night if food was hard to find, but tonight she did not have to hunt. She could return to the deer she had buried in the forest.

The winter of the same year Tawney reached this canyon, she mated with a male from a nearby valley and gave birth to her first litter of two kittens. She fed and raised them for almost a year. Then one morning during a wild, playful chase with one another, the kittens stumbled onto a huge elk quietly lying in some dense brush. Because

they were yet inexperienced and unaware of the danger, one of the kittens was killed by the antlers of the angry and startled elk. Tawney had been too late to save her kitten, but she was able to kill the elk and share the meat with her surviving cub for nearly a week.

Only a few months later as she and her kitten roamed into the outer boundary of their territory, the young cougar was drawn to the scent of a deer carcass. Nearing it, the cub stepped into a heavy steel-jawed trap hidden in the dirt and grass. It grabbed and cut into the kitten's leg. Tawney did not understand the man-made thing that made her kitten cry out in pain. She tried to help the cub by licking its face and head, but there was nothing she could do to end the kitten's torture and fear.

In the distance was the sound of yelping hounds. They raced up the steep mountain slope. With one swipe of her claws Tawney had killed one dog and ripped open a second one before shots echoed through the canyon walls. Something hit a rock near her and then grazed her side. In utter fear and pain Tawney leaped up fifteen feet onto a boulder. More shots sounded. One ended the life of her kitten. Tawney now wanted only to escape from the loud explosions that had injured her and had killed her kitten. She was able to bound up the slope among the boulders and trees. The men with their metal traps and guns and their strange scent were never forgotten.

Tonight, as Tawney crossed over many miles of her home like a ghost in the moonlight, she suddenly stopped. She caught the scent of man in the cool breeze, and lifted her white muzzle and snarled. Tawney turned and headed away from the smell, remembering to stay as far away from man as possible. As she climbed onto a bluff, her eyes, shining in the moonlight, caught an orange light in the valley below. She recognized it as fire, another danger. Her keen eyes picked out movement around the small flames. There were men and a few horses. They were camped in the southern boundary of her territory, but because she could not drive these invaders out, Tawney turned and headed north, back to the valley with her favorite rocky ledge.

As fall approached, Tawney watched her mountains and its animals prepare for winter. In the lazy afternoons of Indian summer, she could observe the deer in the clearing below, gorging themselves to build up layers of fat for the winter months. The colors of the forests began to change. Where aspen trees grew in the clearings, their yellowing leaves made patches of brilliant gold on the mountain slopes in contrast to the dark green of the pine and fir trees. The meadows and valleys were filled with activity. It was the rutting season for deer. The males' antlers had grown large and hard by fall, and Tawney watched the bucks fence with their rivals over groups of does. Years ago, when she was yet a kitten with her mother, two bucks had locked their antlers together while battling. They would have died a slow death of starvation if Tawney's mother had not killed them. The bucks' meat lasted them for over a week.

One morning from across the valley, Tawney heard the bugling call of an elk echo down the canyon. That day she climbed high into the upper slopes where the forest thinned out to only a few trees which grew twisted and wind-bent. Small rodents were busy cutting grasses and stems and piling them into stacks on the sunlit rocks to dry out before storing them in their dens for winter. Ground squirrels were eating as much as possible before they hibernated.

As Tawney lay in the drying grasses and leaves in the high meadow, a golden eagle with a seven-foot wingspread swept down out of the blue sky and brought sudden death to a ground squirrel crossing a rocky patch of ground on the far end of the meadow. Later that day, as Tawney returned to her ledge after eating a rabbit she had found among some of the willows, the skies were covered by gray clouds. By the next morning snow dusted the mountains and it was not long after that the first big snowstorm came to Tawney's mountains. Deer began to move down from the higher slopes to the lower valley where the snow was not as deep. Eagles and hawks also moved. And because Tawney did not hibernate or build up layers of fat, she had to follow her source of food down the mountain.

The ponds were frozen by now, and ice and snow covered a beaver dam in the middle of one of Tawney's favorite ponds. Even though the dam was iced over, the beavers could swim in and out of their entrance beneath the ice and gather the branches they had stored in the muddy bottom of the pond during summer and fall. In a patch of willow trees, a few deer stripped away twigs and pawed down through the snow to reach the old grass.

One night as the snow sparkled in the bright light of a full moon in the crisp cold air, Tawney killed an old doe who had been browsing with several other deer bunched up in the patch of willows near the pond. The doe was weak, like most of the deer that Tawney was able to kill. The deer was old and her skin hugged her ribs. Winters were always harsh for deer and only the strongest survived. By killing the old, the weak, or the sick deer, Tawney helped the rest of the herd. She removed the unhealthy deer and therefore, whatever food was left, was saved for those deer strong enough to survive the winter and breed in the spring. Tawney also helped to scatter the deer whenever she attacked one of them. This kept the herd moving and did not allow them to overgraze only one area and destroy all of the vegetation. In these ways cougars and deer lived together and helped each other.

Tawney's fur had grown thick and heavy for winter and had turned into a grayish tan. The fur of the snowshoe hares had turned into pure white to make them difficult to see in the snow. Yet, Tawney's clear golden eyes could catch the slightest movement in the brush or pick out the small, round black eyes of the hares that stood out against their white bodies. Rabbits became a major source of food by the end of winter when most of the old and weak deer had already been caught by Tawney. Yet in the deep snow, the hares were difficult to catch. Tawney's weight sometimes made her sink up to her low-slung stomach in the high drifts, while the rabbits could jump across the top layer of snowy crust.

Toward the end of winter, Tawney felt the urge to mate and begin a second family. She went into heat and traveled across her territory and into surrounding areas in search of a mate. As she roamed, she left scent trails and broke the silence of the nights with low, deep-throated meows. One night she finally gave a piercing, drawn-out scream that could be heard throughout the canyon in the clear cold air. Nearby, a great horned owl swept down from a high branch and scooped up a snowshoe hare in his talons as the hare had raced across the snow, startled by Tawney's scream.

Soon, Cimarron, a huge male cougar from a bordering territory, picked up Tawney's scent trail and followed it to her. Their courtship lasted two weeks. During that time, Cimarron had to fight off two other male rivals who had come from a nearby mountain. But these males were young and Cimarron's strength and experience gave him the advantage. Because only the strongest males win out over their rivals, kittens will be fathered by only the healthiest males.

After Cimarron drove off his competition, he still was not immediately accepted by Tawney. It took many days before she would allow him near her, even though she purred and rolled on the ground in front of him. Finally, after a long wait that tested his patience and determination, she accepted Cimarron. Within a few days, he left to return to his own home range. He would not see his kittens or even Tawney again until she would come into heat in two or three years.

Tawney returned to her normal pattern of daily life of eating, sleeping, relaxing, and wandering through her territory. One cold morning as she traveled through a clearing, she heard a familiar grunting noise. A porcupine climbed down from a tree after a meal of bark at the edge of the forest. Tawney was feeling pangs of hunger and porcupines were one of her favorite foods. In three leaps she crossed the clearing and reached the porcupine who was clumsily waddling through the snow. To avoid its long quills, Tawney flipped it over on its back with one swipe of her paw and ripped open its unprotected stomach. She ate everything but the skin and quills.

By March there were indications of spring. A warm breeze came up the high slopes of Tawney's mountains. Days were longer and the sun began to melt away some of the snow that weighed down the branches of many trees. Soon, where the sun beat down on the open slopes, brown patches of ground appeared as the snow melted away. By the end of April, grasses appeared on the hillsides and meadows. Three and a half months had passed since Tawney's mating and she had spent the last few weeks searching out a den site. She decided to return to the same place she had used for her first litter.

It was a cave, deep into a narrow gap between large boulders. It gave shelter from the chilly nights and early mornings and it gave protection from other predators, such as coyotes, bears, and foxes, who would kill unprotected kittens. One night, as Tawney returned to the cave after a kill, she felt the pains that told her it was time for the birth of her kittens. By morning she lay with three tiny furry kittens. As each had been born, Tawney licked away the sac of membrane that enclosed them and licked their fur until it was fluffy dry. The kittens were only twelve inches long and weighed one pound. They whined in high mews whenever she licked them with her rough tongue, sometimes knocking them over with her powerful, but gentle strength.

By morning the three kittens were all nuzzled against Tawney's soft furry stomach pushing on each side of a nipple with their tiny forepaws and suckling. The three furry shapes were a creamy tan color with black spots and ringed tails. Their eyes would remain closed for nine or ten days.

The kittens spent the first few days of their life nursing and sleeping. Whenever Tawney came back to the den after hunting, she found them all cuddled up into one furry ball to keep one another warm. As soon as they heard her enter the cave or felt her sandpapery tongue, the kittens mewed in high screams until each found a nipple and settled down to nurse. Soon all three would purr as they drank. Once Tawney had licked them clean to her satisfaction, she licked her own paws and fur and then lay purring in the quiet safety of their den.

Ten days after their birth, with their eyes fully open, the kittens became more active. They played by biting or pawing at one another and made some wobbly attempts to walk, usually falling over. As more days and weeks passed, they learned to walk and then scamper about the cave and finally out into the sunlight. They spent less time sleeping and more time playing by knocking one another over in ambushes

or chases or else by grabbing and biting Tawney's twitching tail. A leaf, twig, or bug became a curious plaything.

Sambra was the littlest kitten. She enjoyed batting about pine cones or pawing at blades of grass. Tawney usually sat and watched her kittens as they romped and played together. Bandit was the male kitten, the biggest and the first to run to his mother for food. Sana was the other female, a quiet kitten but stronger than Sambra and always eager for a playful chase. Whenever one of them strayed too far from the den, Tawney picked him up by the scruff of his neck. The kitten became limp in her grip and allowed her to carry him back to the cave.

When the kittens were five weeks old, Tawney began to wean them by bringing back dead rabbits or squirrels. The cubs were not sure what to do at first. They played with the food until their play turned into a tug of war over the meat. Each kitten finally ate his piece of prey. The next morning as the kittens played outside the cave while Tawney hunted, a huge shadow swept across the ground. An eagle flew close overhead. The cougar kittens gave a shrill whistle of alarm as they raced back into the den. They crouched in the farthest corner of the cave with their backs arched, paralyzed with fear. Tawney heard their alarm and raced back to her den. Only after she licked them, did the kittens relax and then anxiously pounce on the rabbit Tawney had killed and brought back for them.

With spring half gone, most of the deer had already moved up to their summer ranges in the higher meadows, followed by their fawns. As soon as her kittens were able to follow her, Tawney led them up the mountain, finally bringing them back to her favorite ledge overlooking the valley. As the cubs grew stronger they were able to follow Tawney over more and more of their territory. For Sambra, Bandit, and Sana, this was a whole new wide and curious world. Beavers were busy repairing dams, and young birds were trying out new wings. Ducks swam in the shallows of the ponds, and spring and summer flowers speckled the green mountain slopes.

The kittens began to watch Tawney as she hunted for them. One day they watched her flip over a porcupine who had been waddling through the forest. Another day they watched her silently creep up to within leaping distance of a browsing deer. Tawney's twitching tail was all that betrayed her excitement as she crouched motionless in the tall grass. With one fast rush and one spring onto the deer's shoulders, Tawney knocked it over and killed it within seconds by biting into its neck.

The kittens learned patiently to lie in wait until prey was close enough for a short run and a leap. Cougars are not long-distance runners, but their short swift sprints can bring down any animal they can get close enough to. As the kittens wandered with their mother through their territory, they learned the places most likely to find prey. The sound of splashing water meant willow trees along the shore and probably rabbits hiding in the dappled light or deer feeding on the willow leaves. While Tawney was a good hunter, there were always many more unsuccessful attempts to catch prey than there were successful kills. The slightest noise or mistake could send a young buck or doe dashing away in its stiff-legged gait. Now when Tawney was successful, she brought back small live prey so her kittens could learn how to kill.

The summer was a peaceful one for Tawney and her family. She was careful with this litter never to bring them anywhere near the scent of man. By fall the kittens' spots were fading. Their feet and ears looked too big, and their tails were longer and heavier, losing the black rings but keeping the black tips. They were still gangling youngsters who lacked the easy flowing grace of their mother.

As fall once again came to Tawney's mountain territory, animals such as field mice busied themselves with gathering dried grasses. Chipmunks and noisy jays gathered seeds. Trout were spawning in the river across the valley. One afternoon, Tawney and the kittens saw a huge female grizzly bear with her cub fishing along the rushing stream. The bear's light brown hump and shoulders looked even lighter in the bright sunlight. Grizzlies were one animal that Tawney avoided. Once she had given up a huge buck she had just killed when a grizzly ran toward it.

In the hot afternoon of early fall, Tawney, Sambra, Sana, and Bandit stretched out on their rocky ledge. The trees were once again changing colors. A breeze stirred every leaf on the golden aspen next to where the cougars lay. The trembling noise of the leaves sounded as if the tree were almost humming or talking. The cougars looked out over their country—its wild rugged canyons, its boulders, meadows, and valleys. Tawney washed her face by licking her paw and then rubbing it across her white muzzle. Soon there would be frost on the ground and with the coming snows, the deer would move to the lower slopes. Tawney would then follow, this time with her cubs. They still had much to learn. They would probably not kill their own deer for another year, maybe not until they, too, were forced to leave home and find territories of their own. It would be rough for them to make it on their own, but that was nature—only the strongest survived to continue the species.

But for now, in the lazy afternoon, Tawney and the kittens stretched out soaking up the warmth of the sun. In the meadow below, two bucks fenced with their hardened antlers. A red-tailed hawk soared above in the clear blue sky. Finally too sleepy to look out at the wilderness and its animals that lay before them, Tawney draped her long tail around her slender body and lay her head upon her forepaws. Her huge golden eyes became mere slits and finally closed as she went to sleep.

YIP

Yip TROTTED ALONG IN HIS USUAL CAREFREE BOUNDING strides. Halfway along a narrow winding trail, he stopped. His long ears stood erect and his slender nose sniffed the early morning breeze. Satisfied that there was no sign of danger, Yip trotted onward, continuing his morning hunt.

The sun rose over the horizon and cast a golden glow to Yip's rust- and sand-colored fur. His long tail with its dark brown tip hung down as he jogged past a tall cactus. All of his senses were alert to whatever lay ahead of him. Even for a coyote, here in these desert canyons, Yip had survived more than his share of trouble. And he had the marks to prove it. A long whitish scar ran along his shoulder where a bullet grazed him as a yearling. Yip's

swiftness had saved his life when shots exploded from a gun pointed out of a low-flying airplane. The experience taught Yip to take cover from any sight or sound of a plane. Another reminder of a painful experience was his left front paw. Two toes were missing. Yip had been caught in a trap put out by a nearby rancher and had bitten off his toes in order to escape. Each of these events as well as others, taught Yip that to survive, he would have to be a very clever and wise coyote.

Over the years, Yip had also become a skilled hunter. Today as he neared a clump of sagebrush, he stopped and sniffed the ground beneath it where a scattering of fresh rabbit droppings lay. There was a good chance Yip could find the jackrabbit. Yip was not only hunting for himself but for his mate, Rio, who was back at their den standing guard over their three-week-old pups. Yip slowed down his pace and carefully searched for movement among the cacti and bushes. Suddenly, ahead of him, the jackrabbit hopped from one sheltering brush into another. Yip was instantly ready to spring into action, but his eyes caught movement in the brush beyond the spot where the rabbit hid.

Out from a clump of tall grass came a badger. Yip knew this badger too. It was Grouchy, a big old badger who sometimes teamed up with Yip to catch food. Yip was glad for any help today. The jackrabbit took off again and so did Yip and Grouchy after it. The rabbit raced among the desert shrubs, making sharp turns and sometimes leaping more than fifteen feet. Yip was able to keep up with his prey and Grouchy followed as fast as he could. The chase was rather short, ending when the rabbit found a hole in the side of a hill to disappear into.

Yip had seen this happen to him many times before. Sometimes Yip would wait for the jackrabbit to come back out. Sometimes he tried to dig the animal out. But today,

Yip had the help of an expert digger—Grouchy. It took the old badger a couple minutes to catch up to where Yip waited. Grouchy went over to the hole and began digging. Yip meanwhile knew from experience that he should check the other side of the hill and nearby ground for any other hole the rabbit could sneak out of.

Yip did find a second hole on the other side of the sandy hill that was partially hidden by rocks and brush. He crouched down against the ground behind the brush and waited, ears and eyes alert. Meanwhile, Grouchy was busy. Dirt was flying fast from the hole as he dug deeper. Many times when Yip had been unable to dig out a jackrabbit, Grouchy had taken over and caught the rabbit. Other times, if the jackrabbit ran out of a second hole, Yip was able to catch it. In either case one of the predators got a meal out of it. Inside the hill, the jackrabbit was becoming worried and it decided that it better leave by its back door. The rabbit hopped over to the other end of the tunnel and looked out.

There was no sound or look of danger, but there was the sound of the badger at the other end of the tunnel. So the jackrabbit hopped out and in a flash, Yip pounced on it and killed it, once again getting a meal by taking advantage of a situation.

As the sun climbed higher, the desert began to grow hot and many animals had already found a shady spot or cool hole to rest in until the cooler nights, when they would come out and search for food. Grouchy went off down the trail back to his own hole and, after finishing the rabbit, Yip started back to his family. A dove in a nearby tree gave a couple of coos as Yip walked by. On a sandy hill in front of Yip, a fringe-toed lizard dashed across the loose sandy surface and then nose-dived right into the sand, using the scaly fringes on his toes to act like paddles, letting him swim through sand. He escaped from the roadrunner that came to a halt above the spot where the lizard disappeared.

Yip continued homeward and was able to catch a ground squirrel as it darted across the trail. He carried it in his mouth the rest of the way back. As he neared a rocky hillside, dotted with a few mesquite trees and clumps of grasses, he changed his course and walked around the hill until he could approach the den with the wind against him. This way he could smell any trouble at the den. Yip found Rio sitting beneath one of the small trees close to the den entrance. Yip was surprised to see five fuzzy dark brown pups making wobbly attempts to walk out from the hole. This was the first time that they had come outside the hole, even though their eyes had opened several days before.

Yip dropped the ground squirrel in front of Rio who gulped it down. Today Yip and Rio began to wean their pups. Yip regurgitated some of the partially digested rabbit he had eaten. The pups began to lick at it and then they mouthed it down. Rio then took them back into the den where she let them nurse to make sure all the pups got enough to eat. Yip settled down outside in a shallow depression he had dug beneath one of the small trees. It was cool there in the shade. A sparrow hawk flew overhead on the lookout for any lizards or ground squirrels. Soon Rio emerged from the den and sat a short distance away from Yip. The pups were sleeping now. Rio did not spend much time inside the den except to nurse the pups. Instead she kept a watchful eye on everything surrounding their hill. From the top of the hill, Yip and Rio could see anything that might be approaching them from any direction.

Later that afternoon, two of the coyote puppies crawled out of the hole into the sunlight. Scratch and his sister Tumble were the boldest pups and did everything first, set-

ting an example for their sisters and brother. And soon the other pups did follow them outside. Out stumbled Brush, already a much lighter color than the rest. She would grow up to look like her creamy tan-colored mother. Behind Brush was Gray, the shyest pup. He stuck his head into the sunlight and jumped back when he heard Scratch and Tumble playing and rolling in the grass.

While Gray waited in the safe darkness inside the den, deciding whether or not to come out, the littlest pup, Spit, scrambled right over him and out into the new sunny world. Yip patiently sat and watched nearby, panting to cool himself off. Gray finally did come out, more afraid to be alone than to be outside with everyone else. The puppies

became stronger and more confident of their movements
with each small step. Their curiosity kept them busy explor-
ing and sniffing the ground around their home. They pawed
at bugs and grabbed at the grass that moved in the dry
breeze. When the pups became tired, Rio led them back
into the den and nursed them until they fell asleep.

As the orange sun set that evening, the desert animals
began to emerge from their resting places, ready to either
gather or hunt for food. Tonight Rio joined Yip in the
hunt. They traveled to a nearby canyon where a small
stream flowed. Along the course of the stream grew a few
tall old cottonwood trees. A gentle wind rustled their leaves.
Yip and Rio stopped as a yapping and howling came across
the basin. It echoed against the canyon walls. The howl was
a familiar one to Yip and Rio. It was Tucson, one of their

pups born last year. During the winter he had finally established his own territory nearby.

Yip and Rio lifted their noses to the desert moon and answered Tucson's howl. From another direction came the voice of a strange coyote. Tucson howled and yapped again. Yip and Rio joined in until it sounded like a haunting chorus of wails and yelps echoing through the night. But the singing did not last long. Coyotes are usually quiet when they are raising small pups.

The tall cacti were black against the moonlit sky as Yip and Rio trotted across the canyon until they reached Tucson. The coyote was standing over two dead sheep. These sheep had somehow strayed away from their flock and had died. In a nearby canyon lived a sheep rancher, but Yip and Rio never bothered his sheep. There was always plenty of jackrabbits and rodents to eat, but any dead animal found within their territory was used as food.

Tucson came over to Yip and Rio, ears down, tail wagging, and head lowered, showing that Yip was still the dominant coyote. Yip put his two forepaws on Tucson's back and bit the scruff of his neck. Tucson rolled over on his side. The coyotes were happy to be together again. A couple of strange coyotes trotted over toward Yip, Rio, and Tucson. This was Yip's territory, but if there was ever a large amount of food, such as these two dead sheep, Yip did not mind sharing it. So beneath the bright moon and sparkling stars, the five coyotes shared the meat of the two dead sheep.

When they were finished eating, the two strangers left for their own home and Tucson trotted back up the trail out of the canyon. Rio and Yip started back to their den. They had been lucky tonight and had found food easily. Coyotes will eat almost anything. Yip and Rio lived mainly on small animals such as jackrabbits, rodents, birds, dead animals, and even vegetables. Their territory was an average size of about twelve square miles, and there was usually plenty of food. Since coyotes do not live in packs like wolves do, Yip and Rio hunted independently or else together as a team, especially when they had to feed pups as well as themselves. Many hours were spent searching for prey and then waiting for it to come out of a hole or to go to sleep so it would not see them pounce on it.

Tonight Yip and Rio did not immediately return to their den. It was still early, so they took some time to wander and investigate more of their territory. They reached a spot where it bordered on another coyote's range. Yip stopped, ears erect. During the nights, sounds travel easily across the desert. A thrashing noise and then a whine came over the breeze. They crossed over to where the sounds were coming from. Alongside a trail leading down to a tiny stream bed was a coyote thrashing in the bushes. His leg was red with blood. It was caught in a steel trap anchored to the ground by a chain. The coyote was in terrible pain. He jumped high in the air as far as the chain let him, so overcome with fear and anger. He tried to run away, but the chain jerked him back every time. The coyote even began to bite at his own leg that was held so tightly by the trap.

A rancher had put out this trap along a trail he knew coyotes used to go down to the stream. This man thought coyotes were killing his sheep. He did not realize that many of his sheep strayed away or were sick and died because he did not bother to take better care of them. This man wanted only to kill every coyote he could find. He did not stop to think that if all the coyotes were gone, there would be no predator to control the jackrabbits and rodents. Soon there would be too many of these animals and they would eat up the grasses that his sheep needed.

Coyotes had lived in this desert area for hundreds of years in a natural balance with the other animals. They preyed upon the rodents and rabbits and kept their numbers down to an amount that the desert vegetation could feed.

Watching the trapped coyote, Yip remembered the time he had bitten off his toes. Rio and he began to dig at the chain that was buried in the ground. The trapped coyote watched them, whining and panting. Together Yip and Rio dug furiously down deeper and deeper with dirt flying. The chain was held in place by some heavy rocks, so the coyotes had to dig around the rocks until they could move them a little. Finally a couple of rocks began to move and the chain began to come out. The trapped coyote frantically pulled on it. Yip and Rio dug deeper until the chain flew out. The freed coyote ran off into the desert, the trap still clamped to his leg and the chain dragging along the ground. He would probably still have to bite his own leg off to rid himself of the trap. At least now the rancher would not find him and the coyote could find some food and water.

Yip and Rio watched the coyote scramble into the darkness and then they returned to their den. Again they approached it facing and sniffing the wind. Rio circled the den entrance and sniffed the ground. Everything was normal. The puppies began to yip and whine and both parents regurgitated food for them. Afterward, Yip sat atop their hill standing guard. Unprotected coyote pups could be snatched up by eagles or owls, as well as cougars. Yet their greatest enemy was still men like the rancher. To the east, the sky was growing light. A morning dove cooed a good morning and then flew into another tree, its wings whistling as it flew.

Two weeks later, the pups were larger and much more playful. Yip had begun to bring back baby rabbits to start the pups eating whole meat. Sometimes Rio tore some of the meat into bits for the pups, especially for little Spit.

The puppies played most of the time and Scratch and Tumble roamed over much of the hillside. They chased insects and hid on each other.

As the sun set that night and the pups went to sleep, Yip and Rio started off for the evening hunt. Other predators were also out in search of food. An owl flew above them, and not far away, a jackrabbit, startled by the owl, leapt out from beneath a sagebrush. Yip and Rio raced after it. Jackrabbits can leap up to twenty feet in one leap and can outrun any coyote, but tonight Rio and Yip worked as a team. They had learned that some prey such as rabbits run in wide, circular paths when chased. So Yip began the chase and Rio slowly loped behind. Far ahead of her she could see the rabbit begin to run to one side as it started to circle back. Rio trotted over to where she knew the rabbit would race past with Yip running behind it. She hid herself in the brush. In only a couple of seconds the chase reached the spot where she hid and as the jackrabbit passed her hiding place, Rio took up the chase, almost snatching up the rabbit as it leapt past her.

Yip stopped and rested while Rio chased the tiring rabbit. He would have cut across the circle and took another
turn at running the prey down, but Rio was able to catch
it. She brought the food back to share with Yip. When
they finished their meal, they continued their hunt. Soon
Rio spotted another jackrabbit under a mesquite tree. This
time the coyotes used a different trick to catch their prey.
Yip ran far ahead out of sight of the rabbit and then
emerged from a clump of dry brushes about fifty yards in
front of the rabbit. Rio stayed a short distance behind the
tree, out of sight. The jackrabbit saw Yip ahead of him.
Yip began to jump up and down, attracting the attention of
the long-eared animal.

The rabbit was surprised to see a coyote act like Yip.
He stared ahead at the strange behavior. The rabbit was so
busy watching Yip jump up and down, that he did not see
Rio sneak up closer and closer. When Rio got close
enough, she leapt and knocked the rabbit over. Again Yip
and Rio shared their kill. They could regurgitate some of
the food later for the pups, but they also wanted to bring
back some whole meat to help wean the litter.

Yip and Rio trotted off to search for something else.
Along a sandy ridge, Rio nosed out a ground squirrel from
its hole. He escaped from Rio, but she knew what to do.
She chased the animal uphill to the top of the ridge where
Yip waited. When the ground squirrel came over the top of
the hill, it was pounced on by Yip.

The sun had risen by the time Rio and Yip returned
home. Nearing the hill, they heard their pups screaming and
whining in pain. They began to run, but there was a smell
in the wind—the scent of man and also a burning smell.
The coyotes circled the hill keeping out of sight. Suddenly
from beneath a brush jumped Scratch and Tumble, whining
and licking their parents. Yip dropped the ground squirrel

for them and left Rio with the two pups who had strayed away from the hole. He ran over to another small hill where he could see across to his den. The screams had stopped now. The sun was shining on the back of a man kneeling in front of the den. It was the sheep rancher.

This time he had followed the trails of Yip and Rio to their den. The puppies had been playing and Tumble and Scratch had run off after a small lizard. When Gray, Spit, and Brush heard the man coming, they had run into the den. The rancher came over to the hole and built a fire inside the entrance. Then he covered the opening with rocks to keep the smoke and fire inside the tunnel. Soon the smoke reached the frightened pups and it became hard to breathe. The choking pups began to crawl to the entrance. When they reached the fire blocking the doorway, they screamed and whined in pain and terror. These cries were what Rio and Yip had heard. Now as Yip watched, the man took away the stones from the hole and stuck a long hooked wire into the den. He dragged out the scorched bodies of the three dead coyote pups. Yip knew that now it was too dangerous to stay here. He ran back to Rio and the two pups. He and Rio led their surviving puppies to a far corner of their territory where they might be safe for a time.

Three weeks later, Scratch and Tumble were eating whole meat all of the time. Their fur had become lighter in color, turning into a pale drab tone that blended well into their surroundings. Yip and Rio began to teach the pups to hunt small mice and other rodents. One early morning they took Scratch and Tumble with them on their hunt. Today Yip was going to show them how to catch small prey. The pups eagerly trotted along behind their parents, watching whatever Yip did. He showed the pups how to move along slowly until the prey was sighted. The four coyotes hunted among the cacti and brush until Yip spotted a mouse scurrying out of a hole. He froze for a second and then made a rearing leap with his forefeet high in the air. He came straight down on top of the mouse with his forepaws and nose. Yip snatched up the mouse.

A minute later another mouse scurried nearby and Tumble went after it. She tried to leap up and land on top of the mouse like her father had done, but she missed. The mouse escaped down a hole.

Today was also a lesson in patience. Yip saw a kangaroo rat leaping through the tall grasses. The long-tailed rat disappeared into its hole with a mouthful of dried grasses. Yip knew that the rat would probably come back out to gather more grasses and seeds. While Scratch and Tumble watched, Yip carefully crept over to the hole and hid behind some rocks and brush. He waited, ears forward, alert to any sound of the little rat coming back out of the tunnel. More than once, the pups got impatient with what seemed to them to be a long wait. Yip remained motionless until finally the kangaroo rat hopped out. In an instant Yip pounced on it.

Yip and Rio spent the rest of the summer teaching Tumble and Scratch to hunt for themselves. By fall the pups were almost the size of their parents, almost four feet long, including their long brushy tails. They also had their first beautiful winter coats. Yip and Rio had begun to grow their full coats too, after looking rather scraggly during the spring and summer.

Yip tried to teach the pups always to be aware of any sign of trouble or danger, but a coyote is always curious of everything. And sometimes it gets into trouble. One evening Tumble trotted off alone. She found a dead quail and ate it. Then she searched for more food. Along the trail she noticed something strange sticking out of the ground. It looked like a straight stick stuck in the sand. And there was a scent to the top of it. Tumble liked the smell and grabbed the top of the stick. She did not know that this stick was really another cruel device put out by the rancher. It was a coyote getter. Every year they killed thousands of animals.

When Tumble grabbed the top of the tube, it caused the thing to shoot something into her mouth, almost like a bullet. Frightened, Tumble began to run away, but it was too late. A chemical had been shot into her mouth and it mixed with the moisture there to make a poisonous gas. It became hard for her to breathe. Then she went into convulsions. Tumble ran a short way, collapsed, and died. Later that night, Yip, Rio, and Scratch found her—a motionless form on the moonlit desert plain. Tumble was one more victim of man's sad hatred for predators.

Scratch stayed with his parents that winter as the desert became even drier and the nights became cooler. One winter night there was even a dusting of snow on the cacti, but the sun melted it away the next morning. In January, Rio began playfully and lovingly to rub her head against Yip's body. Mating season was beginning. In a couple months spring would come to the desert and the ground would be covered with thousands of bright flowers. Rio would have another litter of pups as the cycle of life began again. Perhaps these coyote pups would survive and grow up to fill their purpose in the desert ecosystem.

From a distant cliff in the cool night air came a long mournful howl. A series of sharp yaps followed it. It was Tucson, only this time there was another coyote with him. Tucson had found a mate. Rio, Yip, and Scratch answered Tucson's call. The coyotes howled back and forth and their haunting desert song filled the night.

SMOKIE

THE BOBCAT CREPT SILENTLY ON PADDED FEET THROUGH the fresh spring woods. Moonlight streamed down through the branches of tall trees just beginning to bud. The dark spots and lines in Smokie's silky coat of grayish brown helped hide her as she crept from bush to bush. She moved slowly through the darkness. Her large golden eyes searched the forest ahead for any sign of movement. A huge, old moss-covered log blocked her path.

Bobcats wander aimlessly through the nights, and Smokie changed her direction by leaping atop the log and following it for many yards over the forest floor. Near the end of the

trunk lay a bushy tangle of plants and old branches. Smokie paused a moment. There was something moving in the brush beneath her. She waited, her long tufted ears forward and her short stubby tail twitching in excitement. The backs of her ears were edged in black but their very tips and undersides were white. These white patches of fur were all that most animals would have seen at night in the dappled moonlight and shadows. *

Smokie waited until a furry brownish shape hopped into the open. The cottontail was instantly knocked over by twenty pounds of fierce strength. Like her larger cousin, the cougar, Smokie killed her prey with a bite into the neck. Then she settled down in the cool still night to eat her catch.

When she finished eating, Smokie wandered along her familiar trails in search of a place to sleep. These woods were part of her territory. It was small compared to the territory of wolves, cougars, or coyotes, but her four square miles provided plenty of rabbits, rodents, squirrels, and chipmunks for Smokie to eat. Not too far away the forest gave way to a meadow. Open places like fields or meadows were good places to hunt and to find rodents. Smokie often hunted there in the tall grasses for field mice.

Her territory was surrounded by rolling hills with some small farms in some of the valleys. Along the edges of her home range were other bobcat territories. On the other side of her woods lived a large male and there was one living along a nearby ridge. Tonight the woods were quiet, but five weeks before, they were filled with the cries and yowls of bobcats during mating season. Afterward the males returned to their own territories and Smokie was left to find a den and feed her kittens alone. Her stomach was now growing heavy as the kittens developed. And tonight after she finished eating the rabbit, she still felt a little hungry.

As she searched for a place to sleep, Smokie walked along a small stream that ran down the wooded slope. There were new ferns growing along it and moss covered the rocks. The water splashed and gurgled as it hit the rocks that formed small fresh pools of clear water near the banks. Smokie crouched down and lapped up some of the fresh cold water. She did not like to get wet, yet she wanted to cross the stream to reach a rocky shelf above the other side. She investigated along the bank and found a log lying across the water and rocks. Smokie used this as a bridge over the stream. Then she climbed up onto the ledge. It was a good place to rest and also keep watch for prey or any danger coming through the woods below her.

Smokie went over to the back of the rocky shelf and lay down. She began to bathe herself by licking her paws and fur and using her wet paws to rub against the ruff of fur on each side of her face. When she was satisfied, the fur on her lips, chin, and under her mouth were shiny white. Smokie yawned as the night sky grew light. Birds began to chirp as she curled up and went to sleep.

Like most bobcats, Smokie spent most of the day sleeping as the sunlight warmed her mossy ledge. Later in the afternoon she lay stretched out near the edge of the rocks, watching the woods around her. Two deer came down to the stream to drink, but Smokie did not bother them. She was content to watch. Only in winter when deer were weak or starving did she ever try to kill one. Sometimes in the fall she would also find deer shot and wounded or dead from careless hunters. It was not easy for a twenty-pound bobcat to kill a two-hundred-pound deer, but in the early spring and summer, fawns were easy to kill if left unprotected by their mothers.

As Smokie watched, the two deer moved off into the forest sometimes browsing on the new plants and the white, pink, and yellow flowers that specked the forest floor. The woods were becoming greener every day now as the days grew warmer. During the day birds chirped and sang and during the night the forest echoed with the croakings of frogs. There was a freshness and an exciting smell in the air after the cold, somber winter.

Four weeks later, it was time for Smokie's kittens to be born. She returned to the same den she had used the year before. It was deep in the forest inside a huge old fallen tree trunk. Mosses, flowers, and long vines helped to hide the entrance. One night, instead of prowling for food, Smokie remained in her den. By daylight there was the sound of tiny mews from within the log. Smokie lay inside purring, curled around two tiny twelve-ounce spotted kittens. They nudged her creamy colored stomach for milk.

The furry kittens were blind and helpless for the next few days, depending upon Smokie for warmth, food, and protection. While they were this small, Smokie did not ever leave them for very long. She hunted within a mile of her den. Like most bobcats, Smokie used many of the same trails every night, visiting spots where she had caught rabbits or rodents in the past. When she hunted, there would usually be a few unsuccessful attempts to catch prey before she did succeed. One night, after three attempts to catch rabbits had failed, Smokie caught the scent of deer and discovered a fawn hidden beneath a bush. The mother doe was gone. Smokie crept closer and closer until she was able to leap onto the small deer and kill it. She ate most of the deer that night and tried to cover over what was left by scratching leaves, branches, and dirt on it. Tomorrow night she could return to the kill and finish eating what was left.

Ten days after the kittens were born, their eyes opened. The smaller female kitten was Buff. She and her brother, Scamp, had begun to paw and bite each other in play.

When their legs grew stronger, Smokie brought them out of the log at dusk and let them sniff, look, listen, and touch the world around their log. For two months the kittens nursed from Smokie until one morning she returned to them with a freshly killed squirrel. Scamp and Buff stared at the furry lump on the ground and cautiously stepped near it. Buff lifted up one paw and slowly touched the squirrel and then quickly stepped back. Scamp sniffed the dead animal. He began to pull at it. As Buff sniffed it, Scamp jumped onto the squirrel and tried to bite into the neck behind the ears, growling at his sister. This was his squirrel. Because Scamp was the dominant kitten, Buff backed away as he pulled and bit into this new form of food.

Scamp did not eat very much of his first meal of meat and he still went over to his mother to nurse. Buff began to taste the squirrel. After eating a little, she, too, nursed.

Smokie finished eating the squirrel and then took her kittens back inside the den as raindrops began to splat, hitting the leaves on the trees. Thunder rumbled in the distance. A cool breeze swept through the woods. Smokie and her kittens purred as they nursed and slept. Smokie also purred, telling them that all was well. They would be safe and dry from the storm while inside their den.

Summer in the forest was a time of plenty. It was the best time of year for Smokie. Her two kittens were weaned. They ate meat now. And finding food was no problem because there were many young rabbits and rodents. High above in the branches young squirrels chattered and played. The woods lay in deep shade as the leaves of the tall trees blocked out much of the sunlight. Some rays filtered down to ferns and flowers, bathing them in a sunny glow. To the young bobcats the forest looked like a lot of huge tree trunks because they did not see the tops of the trees. Some of the trunks were covered with green moss and others looked good to climb.

Smokie had a few favorite trees in her territory that she used to trim her claws on. Near the den was one of them and one day as she sharpened her claws, Buff and Scamp began to climb the trunk. Buff scrambled up to a low branch and looked down at her mother and Scamp, who had jumped back down. Buff was not sure now about how to get back down. She mewed to her mother who looked up and meowed back, calling her kitten down. Buff started down twice and turned back, unsure of herself. Then she started down head first, her front claws grabbing at the tree. She almost lost her hold and began to slide down, so she turned herself around, finding that it was easier and slower to come down backward. When she was a foot from the ground, Buff jumped and ran up to Smokie, who licked her face in reassurance.

At sunset one evening as the woods were filled with an orange glow, Smokie led her kittens away from their home in the huge old log. From now on they would never stay long in one sleeping spot. A bobcat continues to move throughout his territory and has several different places to sleep. For Smokie there was always the danger of an enemy tracking her down if she returned to the same place day after day.

A bobcat's greatest enemy was man. In a nearby valley there was a farm and the man there sometimes came into the woods with his dogs to track down bobcats. Sometimes Smokie could hear the yelping hounds in the far hills as they picked up the scent. Then an explosion would echo down the hills as the man shot the cat out of the tree that it had climbed to escape the hounds.

Even though she did most of her hunting under the cover of darkness, it was even more important for Smokie to hunt at night and hide during the day, because there was always the threat of man. Now, as she led her kittens through the dark woods over rocks and logs, and through vines and bushes, the kittens followed closely, afraid of some of the new sounds and surroundings. Buff and Scamp could always see the white on the back of their mother's ears and the white of Smokie's upturned tail. It helped them follow her.

The bobcat kittens were not the only young mammals following their mother through the forest. A mother badger led her young in search of mice and young birds. Smokie did not bother badgers because they could be fierce when threatened. In the hills there were bears with cubs roaming the woods for berries, as well as skunks and raccoons waddling through the brush with young following in single file.

As Smokie and her kittens moved through the summer

vegetation, she looked for a rocky crevice, hollow log, or large bush where she could hide Buff and Scamp while she hunted. Ahead was the bubbling splashing sound of the fresh stream with the rocky shelf. Smokie led her kittens to the stream. The moving water was a new experience for the young bobcats. The gurgling splashing water was a loud sound, and Buff and Scamp slowly and cautiously approached the mossy rocky banks. As they watched their mother, Smokie bent down and lapped up some water. Scamp went over beside her and pawed at the water. When his paw touched the surface, he jerked it back and shook it. Buff scampered over to them and sniffed at what her mother was drinking. When her nose and mouth touched the water, she jumped back sneezing and shaking her head. Both kittens began to lap up the water. Sometimes they got a noseful, but soon they were drinking the fresh water as well as their mother. Smokie led Buff and Scamp across the fallen log over the stream and up through the rocks to the mossy ledge. She licked their fur and then left them to bring food back for them.

As Smokie roamed along the edge of the woods, she left scats along the boundary of her home range. These droppings let other bobcats know that this was her territory. If a bobcat found a fresh scat, he would know that another bobcat had recently been there. He would usually then change his direction to avoid meeting the other cat. Once in a while, Smokie came across a neighbor bobcat. She usually ignored it, especially if it was one of the nearby males. She was much more tolerant of males traveling in her territory than she was of other females.

Tonight, like most other nights, Smokie relied on the element of surprise to catch her prey. Bobcats are not long-distance runners and Smokie had to find ways to capture her prey as quickly as possible. If a rabbit or rodent escaped from her first attack, Smokie would abandon the chase to hunt for some other prey. Her sense of smell was not as keen as a wolf's or coyote's; therefore, Smokie relied on her eyes and ears. The black tufts of hair above her eartips helped to catch any tiny sound.

Tonight all of her senses were alert and ready to spring into action at any moment. She prowled silently through the edge of the moonlit meadow. There was an old gnarled broken fence along one side of the clearing and Smokie jumped up onto the wooden rail. She sat there looking out across the grass. The night was quiet except for the hoot of an owl in the woods. Not far away there was a rustling noise. A patch of tall grass was moving as something walked beneath it. Smokie's tail twitched in excitement and she slowly climbed down the fence and crept toward the rustling.

A field mouse was scurrying through the grass. Smokie stopped. Then, without a sound, she leapt over three feet onto the spot where the mouse should have been. Her paws just missed the small rodent as it disappeared down a hole. Smokie continued onward through the grass. Before long, another rustling came from ahead of her. She began to stalk the moving spot of grass. This time Smokie did not miss. She clutched the mouse in her teeth and carried it back to her waiting kittens.

When she reached the ledge, the kittens ran to her as she dropped the dead mouse in front of them. It was typical cat behavior for the kitten to want to play with the mouse before eating it. Scamp caught the mouse in his claws and threw it up in the air. Buff began to bat it around with her front paw until Scamp, growling, grabbed the mouse. He dragged it back to the rear of the shelf and began to eat it. Buff watched him and meowed. Smokie left the kittens to find something else for Buff to eat.

This time Smokie followed a different trail leading over a hill and downward toward the valley. Far away there was a light from the house where the man lived. A dog howled, but Smokie knew she was at a safe distance. But the howl was followed by a much closer sound—a thrashing in the bushes and a jangling sound. Smokie slowly crawled forward, stopping at every bush to conceal herself. Off to one side of the trail was a raccoon, struggling to free himself from the grip of a steel leg-hold trap. Every tug at the trap and the chain tied to a tree made the pain worse. Smokie had seen many animals caught or often dead in the traps that the man in the valley put down in the wooded hills. Sometimes she killed the animal for food.

As the raccoon began to bite his own leg to free it, Smokie jumped on him, killing him and putting the raccoon out of its misery. She ate most of the animal and then covered over what was left. Smokie sniffed the metal thing that gripped the leg of the raccoon. The trap had been meant for her, but the raccoon had stepped in it. The man always worried that bobcats would attack his chickens and other animals.

Like the ranchers who hated coyotes, this man did not stop to realize that bobcats were necessary predators and that they actually helped him by eating rabbits and rodents that could damage the man's garden. Like most bobcats, Smokie was afraid of man and she stayed as far away from him as possible.

Not long before, there had been a bobcat that attacked the man's animals. The big male bobcat had been caught in one of the traps the man put out. The cat was able to escape, but suffered with a broken leg that never healed. The bobcat could no longer hunt well enough to survive and he was forced to steal chickens to feed himself. After tracking down the big cat with his hounds and shooting it, the

man still wanted to kill every other bobcat in the entire
area. His traps not only caught bobcats, but also many
other innocent and harmless animals such as the raccoon.
Smokie left the raccoon carcass and started toward the
stream. Along the way she caught a small quail nestling
under a bush. This she carried back and gave to Buff.

The next night, Smokie and her kittens moved to another part of her woods. She also began to show them how to
hunt for themselves. It would not take too much teaching because all the times that Buff and Scamp had played together,
they had used the stalks and leaps they would need to catch
food. Now they began to watch their mother, but they spent
much more time practicing themselves and learning from their
mistakes.

In a grassy meadow the kittens began to chase grass-
hoppers, leaping into the air and through the grass after the
insects. The meadow was a good place to find rabbits, and
Smokie began to stalk one. The kittens watched eagerly.
Catching prey was a series of steps that almost every cat
uses. Smokie's hunt began by walking silently until her prey
was within sight or hearing. Then she froze, motionless, and
waited. She steadied herself and put one paw in front of
the other, creeping forward. Again she stopped, froze, and
waited. Finally in one, two, three bounds, she was on the
rabbit. After eating the rabbit, the bobcat family found a
small hollow log to crawl into and settle down to sleep.

Most mornings were filled with the sounds of birds
singing and leaves rustling in the breeze, but the next morning was different. The woods were too quiet. Instead of
stretching and going back to sleep, Smokie sensed that
something was wrong. She left her sleeping kittens and
crawled outside through the large ferns that hid the opening. Then she heard what was coming, and coming fast—
the hounds. They had picked up her trail from the night

before. The dogs would not be able to fit through the small opening in the log, but Smokie wanted to lead them far away from her two kittens.

As the yelping and barking got closer, Smokie took off through the woods, leading the dogs on an obstacle course through thorny thickets, tangled bushes, and through a swampy marsh nearby. But the hounds kept coming. Smokie tried to use a trick that had helped her escape from the dogs before. She climbed atop fallen tree trunks and ran along the tops as long as possible. It slowed the hounds, but it did not stop them.

Smokie was nearing the spot where the raccoon lay. She ran and leapt past the spot onward down the slope. Off to one side of the trail was a pile of huge rocks. Smokie jumped up through the rocks to the top and looked back. The dogs were reaching the spot where the raccoon was. Suddenly one of the hounds yelped in pain. The other dog just continued the chase, leaving the first dog crying in pain. The hound had stepped into another of the man's own traps.

Now this left only one hound for Smokie to deal with. The dog reached the rocks below where she waited. Smokie proved that a cornered bobcat is more than one dog can handle. As the hound climbed up one of the rocks, Smokie lashed out at him screaming, spitting, and swiping him with her sharp claws. She jumped on the back of the dog and dug into him with all four feet of claws. Both rolled over the edge of the rock down to the ground in a tumbling mass of yelps, screams, and flying fur.

Smokie grabbed the dog's stomach and ripped him open with her slashing hind legs. She killed the hound. There was noise from up the trail. The man was coming and he would have his gun. Smokie bounded off into the forest. Her only injury was a bite on her back leg. Once out of sight and hearing of the man she paused to lick her leg. Then she slowly returned to the log and crawled inside. Buff and Scamp mewed to her and she licked them as she curled up and went to sleep.

By fall the kittens were hunting by themselves some of the time. The forest was changing as a cooler wind swept through it. Darkness came earlier and trees stood covered with gold, orange, and red leaves. The shorter days stirred the animals to either gather food to store, or else to eat more in order to build up layers of fat. Birds ate heavily before leaving on their winter migrations. Acorns fell from the oak trees and chipmunks hid them away in their nests. Gray squirrels buried theirs in the ground. Deer, raccoons, and even bears helped to eat the acorns that specked the forest floor.

Soon the cool winds blew away the dry leaves and the ground was covered in gold. Even though Scamp and Buff were almost as tall as their mother, they still loved to play in piles of leaves. One cold day it snowed and the leaves were covered in white. Buff and Scamp cautiously stepped in the strange, cold wet ground. Buff shook her paws and jumped atop a dry rock. Smokie walked ahead of the kittens. They followed by putting their feet into the footprints of their mother. The forest seemed empty with most of the birds gone. A raven gave a rough caw above the bobcats, but the woods were now quiet except for the cold wind rattling whatever brittle leaves were left on the trees.

By winter Buff and Scamp were able to take care of themselves. A few times they had left Smokie and searched for food alone, sometimes coming back unsuccessful and hungry. But they learned to hunt in the snow, using tree trunks to travel across, or using rocks to sit atop and wait for a rabbit to hop beneath them. If deer were trapped in deep snow, they were easy to bring down. Like cougars, bobcats helped the deer herd by removing the weak, sick, and old. By the middle of winter Smokie was alone. Her two kittens had left in search of their own territories. There were never too many bobcats in one small area. There was not enough food for all of them. By searching out new territories, Buff and Scamp were also ensuring that other areas would have bobcats to help balance the numbers of rabbits and rodents there.

By March, Smokie came into heat again and the cries of bobcats echoed through the woods. Hopefully with a lot of care, wit, and luck, Smokie would live to have more litters, and would teach her new kittens to be true predators.

TORCH

THE FOX MOVED GRACEFULLY AND EFFORTLESSLY THROUGH
the meadow on her slender black legs. As she bounded up
over the hill, her long reddish tail floated behind her. Torch
yowled and yapped her greetings as she ran toward Blaze.
He dropped two mice from his jaws and yapped back to
her. Nearing him, Torch crouched down on her stomach in
the spring grasses and lay her head between her outstretched
front paws. Her brushy tail waved excitedly over her back.
Its white tip flashed back and forth. Blaze came over to
her. Torch sprang up and the two foxes licked each other's
faces. The early morning sun gave a flaming appearance to
the dark red fur on their backs which shaded into white on
their stomachs. Like their legs and paws, the backs of their
ears were black. Blaze licked the white chin and cheeks of

his mate for several minutes. Then he picked up his two mice and both foxes trotted over to the den.

Blaze and Torch moved lightly over the ground. They weighed less than twelve pounds each, but their long, thick winter fur made them look much heavier and rounder. It was the middle of April now and they were beginning to shed some of their winter coats. Torch had lost some fur when she had dug out a new den before the birth of the pups. The two foxes trotted over to the hole lying halfway down the slope of the small hill. The area surrounding the den entrance was littered with scattered dirt and leftover bits of rabbit fur, feathers, bones, and bird feet.

At the bottom of the hill ran a small stream that cut across the large meadow. There were willow trees along the banks just beginning to bud. Some spring grasses and plants were beginning to sprout along the hillside. When Blaze reached the hole, he dropped the mice and called to the four pups inside in a low, soft, mmmmmmmmmm sound. The five-week-old pups scrambled and tumbled out into the light, hungry to nurse. Torch sat down and patiently allowed the growing pups to nurse for several minutes. Meanwhile Blaze walked down to the patch of willows to rest after a night's hunt. He curled up in a furry ball and wrapped his brushy tail over his nose and eyes. In the summer this kept flies away from his face, and in the winter it kept his nose warm.

During the day, Blaze usually took only catnaps, waking up every minute or so to look around him before going back to sleep. His twitching ears showed that all his senses remained alert while he slept lightly. If a ground squirrel moved or chirped nearby, Blaze could come out of his sleep like a coiled spring and leap onto the small animal. All throughout Blaze's three miles of territory, he had favorite places where he slept during the day. These bedding places not only helped to hide the fox but they also were in a spot that the fox could easily escape from if suddenly threatened. Here beneath the willows, if Blaze sensed any danger, he could leap across the stream over the rocks or scramble down along the banks through the thick shrubbery.

When the pups had finished nursing, Torch brought the two mice over to them at the den entrance. She and Blaze had just begun to bring back small mice for the pups, in the slow process of weaning them. The pups were all a fuzzy, dark grayish brown with blue eyes. Their eyes would not change to bright yellow like their parents until they were two months old. But they already had the white tips to their tails—all except Rebel whose tip was black. He was the biggest and strongest pup. Torch gave a soft mewing sound to her pups, encouraging them to take the mice. Rebel began to pull at one and dragged it back down into the den.

Frisky, the other male pup, did not want any more food and began to maul and play with his mother. He pounced on Torch's tail and snapped at the twitching white tip. The two female pups were Streak and Cricket. They both pulled at the other mouse until it became a tug of war. Streak won the tug and dragged her prize down into the den. The foxes' den was made up of several small chambers off the main tunnel which led to another entrance farther down the hill. Sometimes there were several entrances and tunnels leading into the main one. The pups could go from room to room and sleep or else eat their mice by themselves.

While Torch let Cricket nurse again, Blaze woke up and trotted off along the stream bed. He never spent much time at the den except to bring food once or twice a day. Torch made many more trips back and forth bringing food. She usually hunted by night and slept during the day.

While Blaze slept outside all year round, Torch had spent the last few months sleeping inside the den. Now that the pups were growing older, she began to sleep outside.

When Cricket and Frisky went back inside the den, Torch walked down to the willows and napped to the sound of water trickling along the stream. She spent the day sleeping and playing with the pups. As evening approached, Torch trotted off across the meadow to search for food. The weeds and grasses from last year had been matted down through the winter and lay in a thin dry layer over the soil. New plants were sprouting, but they were still very small. Torch could easily see the meadow mice moving beneath last year's layer of grass. During spring, these meadow mice, or voles, were the main diet of Blaze and Torch because they were so easily smelled and heard as well as seen in the fields.

The foxes' diet varied from season to season. They depended upon whatever was easiest to catch. In early spring, the thinly scattered vegetation gave poor cover to the scurrying mice and they were easily caught. By preying on these mice, the foxes kept the number of mice down and prevented overpopulation during the summer.

Torch trotted along in short, jerky movements with her eyes, ears, and nose ready for any sign of food or danger. A twig cracked behind her and Torch stopped, looking back toward the sound. Hearing nothing more, she walked on only to stop again and look back to make sure there was no threat. Once satisfied, she continued her hunt through the meadow. Farther along she paused and stood still. Her long ears had picked up a faint sound. She leapt up and dived down with both paws landing on a spot of dry grass. Underneath was a mouse. She snapped her jaws down on the mouse between her paws, and bit into the head.

Torch ate the mouse in a few gulps, leaving nothing.

When hunting mice, Torch did not try to hide or stalk her prey. She just wandered and pounced or else dug them out of their holes. She would usually eat four or five mice a day, but a large rabbit could be enough food for two days. Yet now she was hunting for her pups as well as herself.

The next mouse she caught, she cached. Torch dug a shallow hole with her front claws and pushed the mouse in with her nose and covered it over. When food was plentiful, Torch and Blaze cached some in one or more places. When food was harder to find, they could go back and dig up what they had buried. Torch returned to the den three times during the night with mice for the pups. Once again they still wanted to nurse before they played with or ate the dead mice.

By early morning all the pups had eaten and Frisky and Cricket were still playing outside the den. Torch sat atop the hill and looked out across the meadow and fields. Today there was no sign of Blaze. Because Torch and Blaze traveled back and forth from the den to hunt at different times, they sometimes did not see each other for days. Torch finally went back down the hill and over to the willows. She circled into the wind and lay down with her head and nose pointing into the breeze so that she could smell anything that might approach her.

In another week, the pups were remaining outside much longer. They liked to run back and forth between the two main entrances to the den. One evening Blaze returned while Torch was gone. He dropped a chipmunk near the den opening. Rebel and Streak both grabbed at it, pulling and tugging while they growled, hissed, and whined. Rebel finally won the battle and dragged his prey into the den. The other pups began tussling and scrambling all over Blaze, who sat patiently for a short time and then left to hunt again.

Even now at only six weeks old, the pups were beginning to show the solitary nature of foxes. They often slept alone in one of the chambers in the den or they often played by themselves. Cricket liked to carry sticks about and toss them into the air. Then she pounced and chewed on them. Streak liked to search around the den with her nose to the ground, uncovering beetles. Because of the litter around the den, there were always enough bugs scavenging for food to keep the fox pups occupied. Streak liked to pick up scraps of food. Beetles would then scramble away from out of their hiding places.

When she was younger, she enjoyed watching the insects, head cocked to one side. Now she pounced on the beetles, pinning them down with her paw and then sitting back and watching what they would do. If the beetle did not move at first, a prod with her paw usually got it moving. If it scurried toward her, Streak jumped backward. Then she would pounce on it again and pick it up in her mouth and chew it. Streak was only playing now but she was also learning how to hunt and feed herself. The pups were learning to feed themselves by trial and error. They spent most of their time digging and chewing on anything that was chewable. Worms and bugs were dug up. Moths and flies were snapped at. Even grass was eaten as the pups experimented with whatever they found. Anything that did not run away too fast or that hurt them was tasted. Gradually the pups learned to connect certain smells with things good to eat.

Sometimes the pups did get into mock battles and group tussles. Frisky sometimes crouched on his belly with his head lying on his forepaws and his tail wagging. It was an invitation to anyone to play. He liked to launch into an attack by making vertical leaps at Streak or Cricket—walking sideways up to them, back arched. Sometimes he slammed against them with his hip and shoulders or else he bowled them over, biting and growling ferociously. Often the other pups joined in with everyone biting, barking, and growling. The pups were often very noisy. When they saw Torch return with a ground squirrel or mouse, they yapped in anticipation. Now that the pups were so big, Torch stood when she nursed them. She was becoming thin and worn down from both hunting and nursing them. The warmer sun had lightened her coat to a blonder color. Large tufts of hair now came out as she shed more of her winter fur. Two weeks later, when Torch returned to the den with three mice, she did not let the pups nurse. She softly mewed to them, encouraging them to eat the mice. Then she lay down with her stomach to the ground, preventing the pups from drinking.

By June, the diet of the foxes began to change. They were adding insects and fruits to their meals. Torch and Blaze knew the places where wild fruit was ripening and where there were wild strawberries. The pups especially began to live on insects because they were so easy to catch. Torch and Blaze ate them because they were so plentiful.

After rainstorms, worms and even frogs could be caught. Sometimes birds could be snatched while sitting on their nests and occasionally eggs were either eaten or cached away. Blaze could hold an egg between his front paws and, after puncturing it, he could lick out the contents without spilling any. Blaze and Torch's pups were already learning to become what foxes were—opportunists. They ate anything that they could find.

One warm clear night in the moonlit field, Blaze heard a rabbit nibbling on some clover. Although he did not usually stalk his prey, he sometimes stalked rabbits. Almost like a cat, he crept through the grass ready to spring. The rabbit was quicker this time, running through the wet grass and disappearing down a hole. Blaze spent some time trying to dig out the cottontail, but the hole was deep. He gave up and continued on through the grassy field, rapidly trotting for a short way, and then stopping with his head cocked to listen. He could hear a mouse over a hundred feet away. And it was not long before he did pick up the sound of one scurrying through the grass stems and roots.

Now with summer's tall grasses in the fields, Blaze could no longer see the mice. He depended upon his hearing. As soon as he heard the mouse, he darted to one side and pounced on the grass. He grabbed the mouse between his paws and ate it. While Blaze's hearing was more important than his eyesight, his sense of smell was the most important sense. It not only detected the sound of prey, but also the scent of danger as well as the smell of carrion. Foxes always take advantage of any dead animals they find. In this way, they not only play their role as predator, but also as scavenger. They help to rid the meadows, woods, and fields of animal carcasses. And whatever foxes do not eat, the crows and insects take care of.

In his role as predator, Blaze lived side by side with

his prey animals, who, being always very watchful, kept their enemies at a safe distance. They stayed far enough away so that if the predator did attack them, they would have enough room to escape. As long as this distance was kept, the predators and prey animals could live together and sometimes seem to pay little attention to one another. Blaze's job as predator was to find ways to reduce the distance that his prey allowed him. Blaze did it by either chasing his prey and outrunning it or by creeping up on it. In either instance, his keen senses were vital to his success. To help his pups develop their senses and their experience, he began to drop food farther and farther from the den. Sometimes the pups would then have to search through the grasses for the food, learning which smells belonged to which foods.

Besides learning the various scents of their prey, one day the pups learned the scent of danger. Torch took them out for a romp away from the den along the stream bed. The pups tumbled in the grass and played with bugs while Torch sat atop a rock pile which gave her a good lookout spot. A breeze stirred the long willow branches. Torch lifted her sharp, slender nose and sniffed. There was no hint of danger. She did not even see it until it was almost too late.

Downwind and behind her came a crackling of twigs close by—too close by. Over the top of the hill came a young boy. Torch crouched down and looked at him. She gave a soft growl and a hiccuping sound. The pups immediately ran for cover under a large bush. Torch galloped away down the stream bed through the cover of grass and bushes. The young boy only caught a glimpse of a slender reddish animal streaming along through the green brush with its long red white-tipped tail floating behind. Meanwhile the pups remained motionless beneath their cover and watched the boy come down the hill and then walk away in the same

direction that Torch had gone. When he passed their bush, the pups caught his scent. They learned the smell of man.

Because their mother had given them the warning hiccuping sounds, the pups learned that this creature was a threat. This time the fox pups had been lucky. The boy would never have harmed them. He was excited to see a real fox running free, and he did not want to hurt it. Yet the encounter served as an important lesson to the fox pups. In the future they would know to run and hide from the scent of man and it would probably save their lives.

Like wolves, cougars, coyotes, and bobcats, the foxes' greatest threat was man. Near and around Blaze's territory, there were farmers and hunters who searched the fields for foxes, gun in hand. The farmers considered foxes to be their enemies because they sometimes lost a few chickens or ducks to starving foxes. But this didn't happen very often, because there were always plenty of mice, rabbits, or even carrion to eat. Dead livestock thrown in a field was often taken by Blaze or Torch. During the fall, hunters shot any fox they saw. These men believed that the fox ate all the small animals that they wanted to shoot. Like any other predator, Blaze and Torch never killed off their source of food. What they did eat was not enough to damage the population of rabbits, quail, or other game animals. The fox, as a natural predator, has kept his prey's numbers in balance long before armed hunters ever invaded the woods and meadows.

There was one more danger that the pups would still have to learn. It was traps. During the fall and winter, some men received money or bounties on any fox pelts that they brought in. They set out steel traps throughout the fields and forests. The foxes that were caught were killed, if not already dead, and then skinned. The long furry, reddish winter coats were then sold and made into coats and clothes for women and men who thought fox fur was beautiful, soft, and fun to wear. They never thought of the cruelty to the foxes or that the fur was even more beautiful on the back of the fox—where it belonged.

By late summer the pups were almost independent. They had learned to sleep outside either in the sun or in a gully or beneath tangled tree roots. Blaze had stopped bringing food to them. He was living and hunting alone again. Torch sometimes brought something, but she never stayed long any more. The fox pups were well furred by now and they had their permanent teeth. They were two-thirds grown, looking very much like their parents. Already they were gaining their winter coats. The playful romps and fights of the pups were becoming much rougher.

In the early evenings after emerging from their resting places, they leapt at and chased one another, giving out catlike screams. The pups were sorting themselves out in social rank. The adult foxes in the area were already sorted out. Blaze was the dominant fox over a wide area and when he mated with Torch, she became the dominant vixen. Now the fox pups were using their aggressive fights to determine who was the strongest and weakest. The litter began to break up, not only because they were able to feed themselves, but because their rough fights began to drive them to become what foxes are—loners.

During the fall, the male adult foxes began establishing smaller territories again. These were breeding territories, smaller than the area the fox hunted within. There could be one or more females in a male's territory. This winter Blaze would be able to mate again with Torch, but this fall there were two females in his territory because Cricket remained there while the other pups searched out their own territories. It was at this time that so many young foxes were trapped or killed as they moved into unfamiliar areas. Of the three pups who left, only Rebel survived to find a terri-

tory and a mate of his own. Streak was killed and skinned
by a trapper who sold her long winter coat. Frisky was shot
by a man hunting pheasants. The hunter cut off Frisky's
long brushy tail to show his friends, and left the dead
young fox lying in a dry, wind-bent field.

As the breeding season drew near, Torch began to
clean out old dens, and she slept in one again. Among the
males, there was much fighting over territories and vixens.
One day Blaze came upon a strange intruder in his territory. The foxes approached and circled each other, flicking
their tails in the other's faces. Blaze and his rival reared up
on their hind legs and put their front feet on each other's
chest. It became a pushing contest with each fox pushing
the other backward. They growled, hissed, and screamed at
each other. Finally the strange fox ran away defeated, tail
between his legs.

Food became scarcer in winter. During the fall the
foxes fed on mice and deer carrion. Hunters sometimes left
wounded deer to run off and die, and Blaze and Torch took
advantage of this. If they found a lot of food at one time,
they cached some beneath the dirt and snow. Their sense of
smell could always lead them back to the spot.

Torch and Blaze also picked up whatever owls left
uneaten. Great horned owls often killed pheasants and grouse
and ate only the head, neck, back, and crop. Torch still tried
to catch mice. She could hear them scurrying along their
pathways beneath the snow. Her trail through a snowy field
zigzagged back and forth as she stopped to sniff at anything
or else to thrust her nose down through the snow after the
sound of a mouse. Usually she came up with only a mouthful of snow.

Because mice and other hibernating animals were hard
to find during winter, Blaze and Torch relied more on cot-
tontails. Winters always tested the resourcefulness of a fox,

and if a fox pup survived his first winter, it was because he had learned to live off of whatever was available.

By late November the male foxes were ready to mate, but the vixens were not ready until January. Then once the breeding season was over, the foxes became fairly quiet again and the boundaries of territories were relaxed. Blaze began once more to hunt in a larger area, his territory overlapping with those of other foxes.

With the bright sunlight reflecting against the snow, Torch's eyes narrowed to mere slits—like a cat's. Foxes are the only canine without round pupils. Unlike wolves and coyotes, who hunt while it is often still light, the fox hunts mainly during the night like the bobcat, and his eyes have adapted to it. During winter, the meadows and woods were a bleak landscape. Sometimes a brown cottontail hopped across the crusty surface of snow or a deer pawed down through it to reach last summer's grasses and shrubs.

The bright colors of fall had faded. Beneath the snow lay the seeds of another spring. Yet from out of this dull gray and white landscape, darted a light-footed animal—its brushy tail streaming behind it and its pointed ears giving it an alert expression. Torch paused on top of the hill. Once again she was digging out sites for this year's den. The wind blew at her fur and parted it along her back as the winter sun shone down, giving it tints of orange and gold. The fox trotted on down the slope—a streak of flaming red over the white sparkling snow.

EPILOGUE

MAN AND HIS FELLOW CREATURES SHARE THIS EARTH. AL-
though man has taken over much of the land, wildlife must
also have a place to live—for we are all brothers. Our life
and their life is precious. The earth does not belong to
man, he belongs to the earth. Man should respect the earth
and all its creatures, never causing harm to the place that
gave him his span of life.

Yet in an overpopulated world with no predator to control our numbers, man has disrupted and destroyed other
lives. He has taken for granted that there will always be
wildlife and there will always be wilderness. But there will
not be—not if man does not start protecting and preserving
what he has left. Man has all the wilderness he will ever
have at this very moment. With each day, the forests shrink
and wildlife is left without a place to live.

The key to the whole problem is education. If each of
us learns about the earth we live in and understands why
there are wolves and cougars, and why we must save them,
perhaps we can make sure that there will be the howl of a
wolf in the wilderness in the future.

BIBLIOGRAPHY

Allen, Durward L., *The Life of Prairie and Plains*. New York: McGraw-Hill Book Co., 1967.

Brook, Maurice, *The Appalachians*. Boston: Houghton Mifflin Co., 1965.

Bueler, Lois E., *Wild Dogs of the World*. New York: Stein & Day, 1973.

Burrows, Roger, *Wild Fox*. New York: Taplinger Publishing Co., 1968.

Caras, Roger A., *North American Mammals*. New York: Meredith Press, 1967.

Costello, David F., *The Prairie World*. New York: Thomas Y. Crowell Co., 1969.

Costello, David F., *The World of the Prairie Dog*. Philadelphia: J. B. Lippincott Co., 1970.

Denis, Armand, *Cats of the World*. Boston: Houghton Mifflin Co., 1964.

Dobie, Frank, *Voice of the Coyote*. Boston: Little, Brown & Co., 1949.

Douglas, William D., *My Wilderness: East to Katahdin*. Garden City, N.Y.: Doubleday & Co., Inc., 1961.

Eaton, Randall L., *The World's Cats*. Vol. 1. Winston, Oregon: World Wildlife Safari, 1973.

Errington, Paul L., *Of Predation and Life*. Ames, Iowa: State University Press, 1967.

Ewer, R. K., *The Carnivores*. New York: Stein & Day, 1973.

Farb, Peter, *The Land and Wildlife of North America*. New York: Time Incorporated, 1964.

Fox, Michael, *The Wolf*. New York: Coward, McCann & Geoghegan, Inc., 1973.

Fox, Michael, *Behaviour of Wolves, Dogs and Related Canids.* New York: Harper & Row, Publishers, 1972.

Gray, Robert, *Cougar.* New York: Grosset & Dunlap, Inc., 1972.

Halmi, Robert, *In the Wilds of North America.* New York: G. P. Putnam's Sons, 1973.

Hopf, Alice, *Wild Cousins of the Dog.* New York: G. P. Putnam's Sons, 1973.

Kirk, Ruth, *Desert—the American Southwest.* Boston: Houghton Mifflin Co., 1973.

Krutch, Joseph Wood, *The Desert Year.* New York: The Viking Press, Inc., 1963.

Kulish, John W. and Aino, *Bobcats Before Breakfast.* Harrisburg, Pa., Stackpole Books, 1969.

McClung, Robert M., *Screamer.* New York: William Morrow & Co., 1964.

McCormick, Jack, *The Life of the Forest.* New York: McGraw-Hill Book Co., 1966.

McNutty, Faith, *Must They Die?* Garden City, N.Y.: Doubleday & Co., Inc., 1970.

Milne, Lorus and Margery, *The Cougar Doesn't Live Here Anymore.* Englewood Cliffs, N.J.: Prentice-Hall, Inc., 1971.

Miracle, Leonard A., *That Cougar Is a Puma.* New York: G. P. Putnam's Sons, 1966.

Olson, Sigurd F., *Wilderness Days.* New York: Alfred A. Knopf, Inc., 1972.

Outdoor Life editors, *Wonders of Wildlife in America.* Waukesha, Wisc., Country Beautiful Corp., 1973.

Rood, Ronald, *Animals Nobody Loves.* Brattleboro, Vt.: The Stephen Greene Press, 1971.

Rue, Leonard Lee III, *The World of the Red Fox.* Philadelphia: J. B. Lippincott Co., 1969.

Rue, Leonard Lee III, *The Mammals of North America.* New York: Thomas Y. Crowell Company, 1967.

Rutter, Russell J., and Douglas Pimlott, *The World of the Wolf.* Philadelphia: J. B. Lippincott Co., 1968.

Van Wormer, Joe, *The World of the Bobcat.* Philadelphia and New York: J. B. Lippincott Co., 1964.

Van Wormer, Joe, *The World of the Coyote.* Philadelphia: J. B. Lippincott, 1964.

John Harris is founder and past president of the North American Association for the Preservation of Predatory Animals. He is now president of the Clem and Jethro Lecture Service and travels the continent bringing environmental awareness through education. Since 1969 Mr. Harris has brought Jethro, Clem, and Rocky, Canadian timber wolves, to over five million people in hopes of destroying the myth of the "big bad wolf." He carries the message that the wilderness must be saved now, while there's still time. John Harris does not recommend keeping wild animals as pets, but promotes the preservation of wildlife in its natural habitat.

Aleta Pahl is a biology and art major at Northern Illinois University. She is a founder of the Society for the Protection of Endangered Wildlife at the College of Lake County in Grayslake, Ill. Aleta has been working with Mr. Harris for several years, using her writing, drawing, and painting to help preserve the wilderness and its endangered animals.